THE EIGHT CONSTANTS OF CHANGE

What Leaders Need to Know to Drive Change and Win

STACY AARON & KATE NELSON

The Eight Constants of Change

What Leaders Need to Know to Drive Change and Win

Printed in the United States of America
ISBN: 978-0-9798009-2-4

Credits
Design, art direction, and production   Melissa Monogue, Back Porch Creative, Plano, TX
info@BackPorchCreative.com

Copy Editor   Kathleen Green, Positively Proofed, Plano, TX
info@PositivelyProofed.com

TABLE OF CONTENTS

INTRODUCTION

Change is constant for today's organizations. But change is hard.

We knew that writing a book about organizational change – change that makes a difference in the way companies work – would be an ambitious undertaking. But when change is successful, it becomes the lifeblood of the organization. However, from our experience helping hundreds of organizations effectively change, we know change can fail miserably.

If organizations want to make effective change, they need to recognize and deal with the eight constants, the eight undeniable truths about change. In achieving any type of change, these eight constants can't be avoided, but we can work with them, mitigate their impact and use them to our advantage.

In this book, we have identified the eight critical constants for leaders to understand and address in order to create successful change.

The chapters that follow stress the need to focus organizational change efforts on the people within the organization, to actively lead change and to harness the power of authentic communications and relationships to fuel successful change.

We hope you find this book useful in your efforts to make transformational change occur within your own organization.

CHAPTER 1

IT TAKES A VILLAGE

Organizations change when the people within them change

It takes a village to change an organization. Not just the chief, not just the elders, but the entire village.

In its purest form, an organization is really just a bunch of people. Sure, there are processes, systems and rules that unite these individuals into groups, but it really just comes down to people. The head honcho can declare change will happen, but an organization can't really change until the people within it change.

When people experience change, they go through a personal transition that affects what they feel, think and do. Understanding these personal transitions helps organizations identify how to secure commitment from the villagers so the change will be successful.

IT'S THE PEOPLE

Organizations are constantly looking for ways to work faster, smarter and better. In the past, the shelf life of any given product or solution was several years, if not longer. But as the world flattens and information flows and competition cranks up to unprecedented levels, obsolescence chases today's products and solutions like a relentless predator. What used to be a good strategy for a few years is now only good for a few months. The future is change.

It is relatively easy for organizations to put new processes, structures and rules in place, but if the villagers are not committed to new ways of thinking and acting, those processes, structures and rules won't yield the expected results.

Organizations often make change an event and describe it in finite terms, such as "the go live," "the closing on the acquisition" or "the product launch," but the change doesn't really happen until employees go through their own personal transition. For the individual, change is a journey, not a destination!

Organizations that excel at making changes with staying power do more than think about strategies, implement process improvements, incorporate technology innovations and respond to market forces. Those companies also consider the implications of those actions and how they impact the people who make the whole organization come together.

Companies good at making changes understand that goals are met through the collective actions of their people. Trying to improve quality? Increase customer satisfaction? Lower costs? Improve processes? Innovate? It's the employees who impact quality of products and services, interact with customers, use resources and create new ideas.

"But," you may be asking, "What about the plan? What about our goals?"

A plan is just a piece of paper if no one is willing to follow it, and a goal is just a number if no one cares about achieving it. Remember, change is about people supporting the plan and striving to reach the goals.

For most organizations, change is now a constant because competition and environmental forces continually drive organizations to change. But, simply surviving change isn't good enough anymore. Companies that can thrive despite change are those that sustain their competitive advantage.

The challenge, however, is the uphill climb for organizations striving to be faster, smarter, better. Study after study tells us most organizations trying to change will fail, and most will fail because people issues get in the way.

A study by the Hay Group in 2001 showed 70 percent of all change initiatives fall short of expectations. Very clearly, the hardest parts about changing an organization rest with people.

In 2005, benchmarking firm Prosci asked representatives from 441 organizations to name their biggest hurdle in effecting change. The most common answers focused on people-related issues: resistance from employees, inadequate senior management sponsorship and cultural barriers, to mention a few.

It's rare to see a project fail because the organization defined the wrong strategy, designed a bad process or built an ineffective technology. It's more common to see a strategy only implemented halfway and, therefore, fall flat on its face.

We've also seen many processes that looked great on paper but did not yield any business value because process workers didn't buy into the changes, but worked around them. We've seen more than a few expensive and complex IT systems that did not yield the forecasted business-case benefits. Why? Because people were not prepared for the new level of discipline or the rigors the systems required.

Once again, the most common mistakes that trip up organizations involve people by not ensuring:

+ they are ready (they know what is expected of them and when)

+ they are willing (they have a desire to be a part of the new organizational direction), and

+ they are able (they have the tools and skills to do what is expected of them) to think and act in the ways needed for change to be successful.

So ... it does, indeed, take a village! People matter. They can make or break an organization's effort to change.

Now, let's be clear. Every single employee within the organization doesn't have to be singing the praises of the change for change to work. However, a critical mass needs to be ready, willing and able to act in the ways required for success in the new paradigm.

WHY PEOPLE MATTER

You're probably asking, "Why do people have such a tremendous impact on the success or failure of organizational change?

By their very nature, people react *emotionally* when asked to think or perform their jobs in new ways. Their reactions to change are driven by human emotions.

Those human emotions involve stages of denial, anger, confusion, and a range of other emotions. Moving through these emotions takes time. Eventually, people move into phases of hope, optimism and commitment to the new ways of working.

ON THE CUSP

As people move through their individual transitions as organizational change occurs, their behavior will vary. So what is really happening at an individual level when people are going through change?

In part, they're seeking to re-establish their own sense of control, understanding and purpose.

When an organization is going through change and people are thrust into their own personal transition, they look for control. They often think that change is happening "to" them … and something – anything – happening "to" them is an uncomfortable feeling for most.

Individuals who don't find outlets to re-establish a personal sense of control will flounder longer than people who are able to focus their energies on small tasks that they can manage.

During change, people try to gain a new understanding of the way things will work and how they can be successful in the new environment.

In the midst of change, people also crave information, often filling in the blanks so that they can fit themselves and their future into the new context. If people don't have what they need to develop an accurate understanding of the future and their role in it, they will fill in the blanks by themselves – whether the information is accurate or not.

People naturally seek sources of support during times of change so they don't feel like they are going it alone. In many cases, the rumor mill will become more active during times of change than during "business as usual." Why? Because people spend more time talking, speculating and commiserating, sharing their thoughts, feelings and concerns during change. If management doesn't provide a mechanism for employees to share their thoughts or speculation in a controlled way, they will do it on their own.

When people set out on a change journey, they'll also try to redefine their purpose. For better or worse, people often tie their purpose to their work. When they sense that familiar work responsibilities may be threatened or fear that they might not be successful at the new ways of working, they start looking for ways to validate their value and their unique purpose. This can manifest itself in many ways, including hoarding information from the change team to make sure they can protect their unique value.

In fact, the human emotions occurring during change are at least as important as other elements of the change. For this reason, emotional reactions need to be recognized and looked after as much as any other element of organizational change.

THE COMMITMENT PROCESS

As people go through these emotions, they develop commitment over time to a new way of working. Through our observations of hundreds of organizations, it is clear that people go through stages of commitment in order to become ready, willing and able to do something new.

But let's have a reality check. We are not talking about asking someone to use the side building entrance while the front entrance is closed for repairs. We're talking about asking someone to think and act differently. We are talking about people who will spend a real chunk of their day doing things differently, making different decisions, communicating differently and thinking about their job or their customers within an entirely different context. For them, change will bring them into a brand-new world.

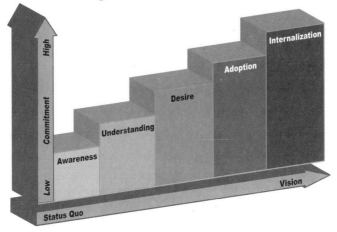

Awareness – people have heard a change is in the works and are aware of the basic scope and concepts.

Understanding – people understand the impact of the change to the organization and to their specific group.

Desire – people understand the personal impact and benefits of the change and are willing to work to make that change happen.

Adoption – people start to actually work in the new ways that are needed for the change to be successful.

Internalization – people make the change their own and think of ways to build on the change to make it even better.

When an organization "flips the switch" on change, the people involved must desire being a part of the new way of working … at a minimum. Once they have some time and practice with the new ways, they can adapt and, eventually, internalize the change.

OOPS – WE FORGOT ABOUT THE PEOPLE …
A Real Life Example

A large U.S.-based manufacturer recently decided the only way they could sustain their growth of new products into the next decade was to start using engineering and design support from India.

The company wanted to double its research and development output but only wanted to increase its staff by a small margin. It made perfect sense – it was unlikely that the existing designers and engineers would figure out how to be twice as productive with the same amount of time and money. Using offshore resources to leverage the people they had was a great solution.

Leaders assigned people to teams and initiated projects to figure out how they could achieve this change. The company spent millions of dollars researching the best practices for working with offshore design resources. They investigated all of the suppliers and took dozens of trips to India to scout out the options in person. They then spent months establishing relationships with their preferred suppliers of design services and painstakingly outlined how people should go about initiating a project with these new "partners" in India.

It all seemed to be coming together!

The VP held a meeting with all of the designers and engineers in research and development and shared the new strategy. He went through a detailed presentation of how the new preferred suppliers would provide offshore design and engineering services. He even gave everyone a handout with the names of the preferred suppliers.

At the end of the meeting, there were few questions, so the VP figured all was well.

A few months later, the VP was meeting with a new product development team and asked them if they had used any of the offshore assistance. They had not. It was not a good fit for their product, the team members said.

At the next quarterly meeting, the VP called a group of his directors together and asked if anyone was using the offshore resources. Apparently only one team was … the team led by the person who had done a lot of the legwork for the VP on how to use offshore resources.

When the company's leaders explored the situation a bit more, they found several reasons their people were not using the offshore support: They didn't understand the need for it, they didn't trust it would work, they thought they might be training these offshore resources to eventually take away their jobs and they weren't being measured or rewarded to do it.

What seemed like a great idea ended up being a complete flop. Why? Because all the "people" elements made this great idea fail.

Several months later, when the company "re-launched" the program, they got it right.

+ They engaged people in helping define how to really make it work.

+ They addressed the fears and questions of the staff.

+ They provided some real examples of products where they had used offshore design support successfully.

+ They gave people the skills to use the resources well by providing them with training and coaches for using the off-shore resources.

+ And they measured and rewarded people for using the offshore resources well.

 **The Golden Nuggets**

+ People make change work (or not work).

+ People strive to re-establish control, understanding, support and purpose during times of change.

+ People develop commitment by going through predictable stages.

ASSESSING PEOPLE READINESS

The first step to effectively changing an organization is to recognize that people are a critical piece of the puzzle for reaching business goals. Because in the end, it really takes a village to change an organization.

Are you and your organization ready for change? Take this short People Readiness Assessment to determine if you have the bases covered when it comes to taking care of the villagers. If you start with lots of "no's" all over the place, then you need to think more about the people. Focus your efforts on changing "no's" to at least "somewhat's". The most successful changes will be all "yes's" when the change takes effect.

People Readiness Audit	Yes	Somewhat	No
Do people know what the change is?			
Do people know the basic scope of the change?			
Is there a clear understanding of the need for change?			
Do people understand how the organization will be impacted by the change?			
Do people understand how the change will benefit customers and other groups?			
Do people know how they personally will be impacted by the change?			
Are people excited about the future?			
Are people willing to do the work necessary to make the change successful?			
Does the organization have the skills/ competencies to get the job done?			
Are people actually trying out or doing the new things that are needed?			

Adapted from *The Change Management Pocket Guide: Tools for Managing Change* (Change Guides LLC, 2005)

AN OBJECT AT REST TENDS TO STAY AT REST

Resistance is inevitable

An object at rest tends to stay at rest. To change is to learn something new, to think differently, to act differently and to move in a new direction.

Great ideas, great people and great projects have fallen victim to resistance to change. Resistance to change means people are working hard to protect the status quo. When people who resist are ignored or pushed aside, they become formidable opposition.

In order to succeed at change, resistance and the people who resist should be viewed differently. Here's why:

> Resistance is a natural part of the change process and exists in many forms. People resist for different reasons and in different ways.

To master change, you must first understand the personal, structural and physiological reasons people resist. When you understand resistance, you can learn to expect it and even use it to your advantage. Understanding and managing resistance is critical when you are promoting change.

IT'S PERSONAL

People have personal reasons to resist change. The most common personal reasons we have encountered are:

1) habit and fear of the unknown,

2) threat to expertise or prominence, and

3) differences in attitude and absorption rates.

1. Fear of the unknown is related to the human tendency to form daily habits. An employee understands the "today" at work. Most likely, she may park in a similar place every day, take the same route to her desk, work near the same colleagues, access data on her computer the same and go about her day in a fairly routine way.

Her day is predictable. Even "surprises" probably come from the same people such as her boss or a regular customer. Predictable daily events over time become comfortable.

When a leader announces a change, whether it is a new computer system, moving to a cross-functional team environment or even a move to a new building, it can be scary or, at the very least, worrisome.

The announcement of a change threatens this comfortable "today" the employee knows and introduces a "tomorrow" that she doesn't know.

2. **The second personal reason an employee may resist change is because it threatens his expertise or prominence.** This relates to changing someone's job or perception of himself.

Here's an example: Joe works on the shop floor. He works a particular machine that stamps out fenders. This machine is tricky and breaks down a lot. Joe seems to be the only one who can fix it. He also has the best rate for quality compared to the other shifts that use the same machine.

When you ask Joe how he does it, he usually just smiles and says, "Joe magic." Joe obviously takes a lot of pride in the fact he is #1 on this machine, and he'd like to keep it this way.

Now imagine how Joe would feel if he attended a meeting where the CEO announced that the line was going to be further automated and his beloved machine was going away. This announcement creates a threat to Joe's expertise. He also may worry about losing value to the company once his machine is gone. Joe may initially resist this proposed change because it threatens his level of expertise.

Threat to prominence is based on the perception that something someone values will be taken away.

Put yourself in the shoes of a leader who values the size of the budget, the number of direct reports, the title or even the location of the office. This leader may resist any change that threatens one or more of these things.

Suppose the CEO announces a restructuring and office redesign. You've worked hard under the old system for 15 years. You've worked your way up, from intern to VP. You think you've earned the corner office and the high-level responsibilities of your job.

Under the announced plan, the organization will be more of a matrix than a traditional hierarchy. Some of your most valued employees will no longer be yours but will be shared on cross-functional projects.

With the new plan, you feel a loss of control and power. In addition, all corner offices will be turned into common areas for team work. At first, this is a bit too much for you to take and your knee-jerk reaction says, "Whoa, no way!"

3. **The third personal reason to resist change has to do with attitude and absorption rates.** Some individuals accept change more readily than others. Some embrace change and innovation while others take a wait-and-see approach. Some even say to whoever will listen, "there is no way this place can pull this off."

We've all seen groups embracing change, while other groups take more time to accept a change. We've even seen the laggards who sometimes opt out – quitting the company or being asked to leave.

A LITTLE HELP AND UNDERSTANDING

Along with personal reasons for resistance, there also are structural reasons. A motivated and hard-working innovator still may not be able to change because of the lack of support around him.

Structural reasons include:

    1) lack of skills or information,

    2) mismatched evaluation system,

3) lack of resources, rewards or recognition or,

4) lack of appropriate reporting or collaborative relationships.

While these structural reasons all sound like formidable barriers, they can be overcome. Yet, we have seen organizations miss goals due to structural reasons.

For example, a worker who is evaluated on volume but is supposed to pay attention to quality gets a mixed message. Do they take a little extra time to ensure quality? If they do, volume will decrease. Since they are being evaluated on volume, they stick to volume and quality does not improve.

Finally, there are also physiological reasons people resist change. An article, "The New Neuroscience of Leadership" written by David Rock and Jeffrey Schwartz (*Strategy + Business*, Issue 43), explains how the brain must work much harder, taking more physical energy to do new things.

Resistance assures no new work will be required. In their article, Rock and Schwartz state that "after just a few months of learning to drive a car, people can typically drive "without thinking." If they then try to drive on the other side of the road, say in another country, the act of driving suddenly becomes much more difficult.

We all can relate to this because driving becomes automatic. We've all heard people say they don't even remember driving to work.

Compare that to driving to a new location where you need directions and a map. It takes more effort. This analogy can be translated to the work environment. If employees have daily habits and are suddenly asked to make new habits, the brain must work harder. This goes against the brain's natural inclination to conserve energy.

RESISTANCE IS GOOD

So, resistance to change is inevitable and comes in many forms and for many reasons. Because of that, resistance should be proactively managed and recognized early. When leading change, think of people's resistance as an opportunity to learn.

Create an environment of open communication that allows people to voice their concerns. Only after hearing the reasons for resistance can you determine if it is critical to the project's success. Once you listen, you need to do one of three things to respond to the resistance. Determine if it is:

1) a legitimate concern that needs further investigation,

2) a misunderstanding you can clarify,

3) unrelated to the project success.

You may encounter all three scenarios, but pay closest attention to the first because it is the most important.

1. Valid concerns about the change are important. If those concerns surface late in the project, momentum can be lost and the project can miss its original timeline or even be shelved all together. Leaders and managers can't know it all. Workers have valid concerns and their input makes the end result better.

2. Misunderstanding is very common and can be addressed with a good communication and involvement strategy, which is covered in chapters 6 and 7.

3. The third reason, unrelated to your project, may need to be documented and forwarded to the appropriate person or put on the back burner.

Only when you understand the structure and energy behind resistance can you do something about it.

In some cases, people may not be open and honest or may not even realize why they are resisting. In this instance, you need to be persistent and ask a lot of questions. With a sound strategy for uncovering and addressing resistance, you increase the chance of project success.

ASK AND YOU SHALL RECEIVE ...
A Real Life Example

The company was changing from a paper record-keeping system to an electronic record-keeping system. The project leaders proactively engaged the end users, holding regular update meetings and employing a good communication strategy, including making the rounds in different departments.

Concerned that resistance wasn't being brought to the surface, they started incorporating Q&A sessions and had us – an unbiased third party – survey the audience to uncover perceptions and concerns.

Things were going fairly smoothly until we went to the billing department. In this session, the project leader talked about how employees from the billing department had been involved in creating the data screens for the last few months, so the department should be happy with the end result.

As she relayed this information from a recent update meeting, several in the audience challenged her, saying, "That's not true."

They had been approached only this week and were unhappy with the draft screens.

The project leader was taken aback since the audience's information ran counter to what she had been told. Not only was there resistance from the billing department, but more information was needed to undercover the cause of the misunderstanding.

Several meetings ensued until it was discovered that the IT department had been misrepresenting their work. Instead of following the project plan, they did things their way without telling anyone. Obviously, they were resisting their part of the plan.

Because the project leaders had started this dialogue with the billing employees early, the issue was uncovered three months before the new process "went live," allowing time to recover and make adjustments.

If they had not taken this proactive strategy of uncovering resistance, the billing department's transfer to electronic documentation would have been delayed, hurting morale and project credibility.

 **The Golden Nuggets**

✦ There are personal, structural and physiological reasons to resist change.

✦ People adopt change at different rates.

✦ Resistance must be brought out in the open so everyone can better understand and address the change-related challenges.

UNDERSTANDING RESISTANCE

This exercise raises the awareness of the group (all levels of the organization) and helps them think about their own personal role in changing themselves and others:

1. Divide people into groups. Using flip charts, have them answer this question: "Why do people resist change, and how do they resist?"

2. After they've talked about resistance in general, ask them to each write down a time they have personally resisted change and why they resisted.

3. Ask them what resistance currently exists or what resistance they expect for your project.

4. Now you can come up with a plan to engage key people in addressing current resistance and uncovering other areas of resistance.

CHAPTER 3

OLD TREES HAVE DEEP ROOTS

*Commitment to the past
hinders change in the future*

Have you ever pulled weeds? Weed roots are a couple of inches long and pull out easily.

Have you tried to move a tree? It's impossible, unless you have heavy equipment. Tree roots grow two to three times the height of the tree and go several feet deep into the earth.

Organizations can be like old trees, rooted in tradition in the same spot and the status quo. We have found three forces that help determine how deep-rooted an organization is. These forces are:

1) the employees' perception of the company's current state,

2) the number of changes implemented over the past few years and their track record,

3) cultural values, beliefs and exhibited behavior.

These forces can help or hinder a change. Therefore, it is critical to understand these forces, their challenges and the potential benefits they represent.

PERCEPTION IS REALITY

For change to be possible, people have to believe that the change is worth doing – either because there is something wrong with the way things are being done or that there is a future that is much brighter than today. The idea of change can be a hard sell if the people believe everything is great just as it is.

Perception is reality. If the company seems fine, employees will think there is no need to change, even if the company must change to be competitive and survive.

If employees see leaders driving expensive cars, new computer equipment being installed and consultants roaming the halls, they conclude that all must be well. These cues say, "the company is spending a lot of money and is successful." They also promote the perception that the status quo is great – and these roots run deep.

In this situation, the employees' perceptions must be changed before their actions will change.

To create this change, the current situation must be reframed in a way that gets the employees' attention. This reframing will get people unstuck, get them to pay attention and, most importantly, get them to care about new ideas.

Reframing also helps employees recognize there is something wrong with how things are done now and change is a top priority.

To change their perceptions, employees need new information, new cues and new messages.

Much has been written about this reframing, creating a sense of urgency and developing a case for change. To change employees' perceptions and motivate them to think and act differently, three elements should be included:

1. **An articulated vision.** Here's where the company is headed and what it looks like – not just from an overall perspective but from a worker perspective.

2. **A description of future opportunities.** Here's what to expect if we achieve this vision. Here are the new opportunities, such as introducing new products, expanding globally, business growth or job creation.

3. **A description of consequences.** Here's what will occur if we don't reach this vision. Here are the consequences, which could mean decreased market share, cost cutting or layoffs.

These elements should not be seen as threats or an impossible dream. In the reframing process, leadership should be clear and honest. An initial jolt to change perception is critical in getting everyone's attention.

But, on the other hand, what if it is known throughout the organization that sales have decreased, budgets are being cut and financials are poor? Then, the stage is already set for a message of change because the employees' perceptions are aligned with reality.

In this scenario, the employees may even be waiting for leadership to step up and tell them what needs to be done to improve the company and protect their jobs. However, while the leaders still need to communicate their case for change, this audience will not be as surprised as employees of the company where everything seems fine. That's because the soil around these roots is looser and the roots aren't so strong.

FLAVOR OF THE MONTH

There are usually three typical scenarios, or flavors, that describe past changes in an organization:

1) "Plain vanilla" – nothing new has been introduced and nothing much has changed for a long time.

2) "Rocky road" – change has been tried in the past and unsuccessful.

3) "Peachy" – several initiatives have been introduced over the past few years and most have been fairly successful.

If nothing has changed in your company for a long time, change will be hard. The organization's flavor might be described as "plain vanilla." The longer a group, individual or situation has remained static, the greater the investment in the current way of doing things and the greater the resistance to change.

The fact that people are proud of what they do and how they do it is a great thing – except when you want to change it.

At the other extreme, you'll find that employees can get accustomed to change and even thrive in that environment. However, employees unaccustomed to change will be surprised and possibly shocked when something different is introduced. As change occurs, they will need to learn a new competency – a competency of coping during times of change. This competency takes time to build, and until employees learn to cope with new or different ideas, this company will be slow to change.

On the other hand, if the CEO has a habit of announcing the "initiative of the week," change will be hard for different reasons. These roots run deep, as well. This is "rocky road."

These initiatives seem to arrive with a splash and then disappear, never to be discussed again.

When these "flashes in the pan" or "weekly initiatives" never achieve traction, they are failures – and there are many direct and indirect costs associated with failures. Direct costs include wasted resources, unmet objectives and failed strategies. The indirect costs of failure, which are just as critical, include lower morale, less confidence in leadership, increased resistance, increased cynicism about future initiatives and increased concerns about job security.

When a company has a history of failure, it is critical to position the new initiative as different from the past. There are many ways of doing this, including how:

1) the audience is approached and included (chapters 4, 6 and 7),

2) leadership acts (chapter 5),

3) the change is sustained (chapter 8).

If a company has a recent history of success and the proposed change is a good one, the change will be more easily accepted. This creates the "peachy" scenario.

Change always takes hard work, but this "peachy" type of company has employees who are becoming accustomed to change and know it makes the organization better in the long run. These employees are building a change competency.

The roots are there, but it is a young tree with shallow roots near the surface.

THE CULTURE FACTOR

Culture impacts an organization's ability to change and the speed of putting these changes into place. As consultants, we've observed certain elements of an organization's culture that can either improve or hinder the organization's ability to implement change.

Culture is shared beliefs and values demonstrated in behavior patterns. Culture is visible every day in what people in an organization do and say. There are many ways to define and demonstrate culture, but we've found the following elements and activities say much about an organization's culture:

+ the messages leaders send with their words and actions;

+ how people communicate;

+ how people view conflict and whether it is encouraged or squashed;

+ how employees are supported, both professionally and personally;

+ how people learn and share knowledge;

+ what types of behavior is reinforced;

+ and, of course, how they view change.

When we work with a company, we find employees are more accepting of change when these characteristics are present:

+ managers and leaders have a collaborative approach to decision-making;

+ managers have a proven track record of doing what they say and are trusted;

+ employees believe change is possible (lack cynicism);
+ people at all levels of the organization tend to be action-oriented and are open to new ideas and dialogue;
+ learning is valued and promoted;
+ there is a belief that things can be better.

Whatever the change, it will be more successful if it is consistent with the company's beliefs and values.

An organization we recently worked with had immaculately groomed gardens around its headquarters, beautiful marble floors throughout their offices, and encouraged the use of the most elite consulting firms around. When they began an effort to cut costs by adopting lean work processes, the organization was completely confused. They had a hard time even understanding what cost cutting meant given their pattern of spending.

Furthermore, there are some cultural attributes that make any kind of change hard. In a culture where leaders can't be questioned and employees don't trust management, change will be difficult. In cultures where no one makes a decision for fear of making a mistake, change probably won't happen easily, either.

Cultures that are inwardly focused also don't change well. The people in these inwardly focused organizations don't have a good understanding of the outside world (customers, competitors and their industry). If employees or leaders protect the status quo or are closed-minded, don't count on change happening.

There are many organizational forces that encourage or hinder change. Employee perceptions, the level of success of past initiatives and cultural characteristics all play a role in how change is received. These attributes need to be considered when implementing change.

Improves ability to implement change	vs.	Hinders ability to implement change
✦ Collaborative leadership style		✦ Authoritarian leadership style
✦ Trust in management		✦ Distrust of management
✦ People believe change is possible		✦ People believe change is not possible
✦ Action-oriented		✦ Analysis paralysis
✦ Openness to dialogue and ideas		✦ Close-minded
✦ Unease with current state		✦ Value status quo
✦ Learning organization		✦ Inwardly focused
✦ Consistent with beliefs and values		✦ Not consistent with belief and values

Before trying to implement change, it's important to find out how deep these roots run in your company.

CULTURE STARTS WITH LEADERS ...
A Real Life Example

A mid-size service organization is about to reorganize and change its core business processes. The organization has 80 employees who are generally young and energetic. The organization has grown quickly; the former ways of working are no longer effective.

The leaders of the company are the founders. They expect to be involved in all decisions that happen in the organization and have a hard time "letting go." The founders tend to tell people what to do rather than work collaboratively to get things done.

Given that the founders have far more experience than the staff, they think that they should direct most of what happens in the organization so clients get the best service possible. Managers used to present new ideas to the founders but quickly learned they would be shot down. Now, managers focus on doing what is dictated.

In general, the people who work at this company are eager to see improvements and are excited to win in the marketplace. However, their hesitation to do something new or different sometimes hinders competitiveness. They are action-oriented and take great pride in the organization.

The founders asked us to assess what elements of their culture could hinder their growth and what strengths they should further capitalize on.

After reviewing the results from their culture assessment, the founders realized their behavior was setting the tone. With this in mind, they started pushing decision making down to the next level of management.

They asked key managers to take a more visible role championing new ideas and initiatives. They pushed back when asked to make a decision, simply saying, "You decide." Social activities were incorporated into the calendar and attitudes slowly improved. Employees were encouraged, and the business started to grow. Not without its bumps of course, but they are on the right track to succeed and have implemented changes successfully.

Culture change takes time, but it can be done with a vision for the future, the right leadership, an understanding of the challenges and a plan for change.

The Golden Nuggets

✦ If employees perceive that nothing is wrong, nothing will change.

✦ The success or failure of past initiatives impacts how people view future initiatives.

✦ Culture can hinder or support change.

HOW DEEP ARE YOUR ROOTS?

This exercise requires participants to be honest. Sometimes doing the exercise with peer groups provides the best results. Otherwise, participants can be intimidated when their boss is in the room. Use a neutral party, possibly from outside the organization, with strong facilitation skills to manage the group.

1. In the first group of meetings, divide people into groups and have them answer these questions:

   a. How well is the company doing financially and compared to its competitors? Why do you think this? After discussing the responses, have the group come up with suggestions on how to address any misperceptions about the company.

b. Does this organization launch a lot of projects? Support your answer. If the answer is "yes," are these successful? Why or why not? After this discussion, have a group come up with "lessons learned" from past project launches.

2. In a follow-up meeting, bring representatives from all the groups together to compare results. Results usually differ depending on the level or department.

a. Have them discuss reasons for the differences.

b. Have the merged group reach a conclusion about how deep the roots run in the company. Have them come up with ideas on how to improve future change initiatives.

CHAPTER 4

GET TO THE HEART OF IT

Connecting to the head **and** the heart builds commitment

Individually and as a group, people are not rational beings. When considering change, remember – there is an **emotional** connection necessary for people to commit to new ways.

Unfortunately, change is not always viewed as rationally as we would like. When people experience change, they go through an emotional transition. And, because there is emotion involved in change, there also is a need to appeal to the heart as well as the head.

But before we move on, let's clarify one thing: Connecting with people and appealing to their heart is not about coddling them and singing "Kumbaya." Connecting means helping people develop a belief and mindset that will drive the behaviors the organization requires.

Connecting requires an ability to change peoples' perception of what is happening rather than just focusing on the hard-and-fast facts. It requires using and recognizing "tacit" or unspoken communication. And real connection requires leaders to define what the change will mean for each individual rather than just the organization.

THE INVISIBLE LANGUAGE

Much communication happens in the workplace, and not all of it is visible. "Tacit" communications and interactions, for example, are understandings that are shared without being openly expressed. These invisible communications are significant drivers of professional productivity.

Communication within an organization includes messages that are neither verbal nor written. These communications and interactions drive thoughts, feelings and choices about projects, coworkers and purchases. They drive what information, ideas, products, services and people will be embraced or ignored. These messages are subtle but can drive an overall course of action.

Dr. Charles Galloway, an expert in nonverbal communication, said, "Exchanges without words – such as looks, glances, agreements and actions that go beyond the obvious – weigh heavily on decisions and judgments."

He continued by saying, "Decisions are made every day, based on unstated agreements among workers about relationships with each other and their managers ... it's a silent language."

How many times have you caught the eye of a coworker during a meeting? Without words, you knew you both were thinking the same. The message you exchanged with that glance could have meant, "This is a ridiculous sales goal that we can't make and this manager doesn't know what she's talking about."

At the end of the meeting, you both walked out of the room feeling little commitment to the sales goal, supported with the knowledge that at least one coworker felt the same as you (even though nothing was ever said).

Tacit interactions are subtle. Yet, these communications play a major role in how employees relate to each other and the decisions they make every day. Paying attention to invisible or tacit communications and interactions help you better understand why these relationships and decisions occur.

When engaging people's hearts and minds, being aware of tacit communications is necessary because these invisible messages shape deep-seated beliefs that are hard to counter or combat. These beliefs may be wrong, but if you don't know they exist, it is hard for you to help people change them. When tacit understandings are driving behaviors, connecting emotionally is even more important so that we can dispel any inaccurate unspoken beliefs.

THE INVISIBLE LANGUAGE IN ACTION ...
A Real Life Example

Two new managers in an organization were adjusting to their roles. Even though they had the same titles and similar responsibilities, their perspectives couldn't have been more different.

Joe had failed repeatedly to collaborate with other parts of the organization. He was frustrated by the extra effort it took to get others to pay attention to issues. He wondered why it took so much effort to get others on board for projects that were in the company's best interest.

Steve, on the other hand, was being invited to participate in other department's meetings. He was working well across groups, received information readily and made decisions well with others. Steve was having great success, while Joe seemed to have invisible walls around him. Who was getting more done? Almost certainly Steve.

It seemed understood by coworkers that Joe's ideas and issues were not important. It's possible no one ever said it out loud, but people were acting on that tacit knowledge.

For the most part, people ignored Joe. They made his projects a low priority, they didn't find time to meet with him, and they waited to return his e-mails. In contrast, it seemed understood that Steve was a worthy contributor. He was included and listened to. Again, it is doubtful that this was explicitly talked about, yet everyone knew it.

This tacit knowledge about Joe and Steve impacted their relationships and productivity. And while this behavior went on silently, it was hard for Joe to really do anything to change the dynamic that had developed around him. Eventually, Joe quit because he was frustrated that he couldn't get things done.

The tacit understandings of the people in the organization drove the belief that Joe was not important. Attitudes were formed and behaviors followed.

If Joe had recognized early on that there were forces at play other than the explicit conversations he was having, he may have been able to "read between the lines" and possibly get to the core of why he was being disregarded.

CHANGING REALITY

Perception is reality. What a person **believes** to be true **is** essentially true for them. Perception is shaped by experiences, motives, interests, expectations and a whole host of other factors. When it comes to change, the most important thing to know about perception is that it influences people's attitudes and behaviors.

Connecting to the heart rather than just the head helps change deeply rooted perceptions that can really drive behaviors. Changing perceptions is not easy, but by using thoughtful influence and persuasion, it can be done.

Using influence and persuasion does NOT mean begging or forcing. It means moving people to action through developing a shared view. This requires careful preparation, appropriate framing of arguments and finding the right emotional match for the audience.

This doesn't mean smoke and mirrors or slight of hand. It means being up-front and honest about your intent to influence behavior.

Building credibility, framing goals and using appropriate reinforcements will set the foundation to connect emotionally with people.

Many leaders rely on their expertise to build credibility. That's a great start. Having a proven track record for making good decisions and being well informed gets the ball rolling. And, don't forget, your relationships, reputation and personal attributes will also help build credibility.

A person who is known for having strong character and being truthful will have much more success influencing and persuading others than someone who doesn't have the same reputation.

When framing goals, find common ground with the people who need to be persuaded. Putting yourself in their shoes will help you gauge what is important to them. Describe the change in terms that emphasize advantages your specific audience will value and appreciate.

And strive to connect emotionally with people. Share your personal emotional commitment to the position you are advocating. Show them your commitment is not just in your mind but in your heart, as well.

There are, however, some fatal flaws that people make when trying to influence people. Keep your eyes out for these mistakes to avoid when changing perceptions.

Common mistakes in influencing people

1. Attempting to make your case with an up-front, hard sell.
   + A strong position at the start gives potential opponents something to fight against.
   + Present your position with finesse and reserve.

2. Resisting compromise.
   + Persuasion is a process of give-and-take.
   + People need to know that a persuader is open to their concerns.
   + Compromise can often lead to more sustainable shared solutions.

3. Thinking the secret of persuasion lies in presenting great arguments.
   + Arguing your position is only one part of effective persuasion. You still need to rely on other tactics, like connecting emotionally and communicating effectively.

4. Assuming persuasion is a one-shot effort.
   + Persuasion is a process that involves listening, testing a position and compromising. It is not an event.

WHAT'S IN IT FOR ME?

When it comes to change in an organization, most people want to know, simply and honestly, "What's in it for me?" This is human nature. Sure, I want to know how the organization is going to benefit. I want to know how great the change is going to be for our customers ... but when the rubber meets the road, I want to know, "What's in it for me?"

A large medical equipment manufacturer that produces products in Mexico has a great work force of committed employees who travel from other areas of Central America to work for the big manufacturer.

Last year, the company came up with a great new product that had the potential of revolutionizing medical care and saving countless lives.

When leaders of the company were ready to roll out the new product (along with the new production lines and processing techniques the product would involve), they wanted their employees to know the importance of this new product. By doing so, they hoped to motivate the employees to readily adopt the new manufacturing techniques.

To achieve this, the leadership had professional video clips of people who had been saved by the device. There were also tear-jerking pictures of those suffering who could be helped by the new product. And there were moving tributes about those who had suffered and who could now be saved by the new product.

All in all, it was a motivational campaign for the folks in the U.S. who were selling the product to doctors and hospitals. Every time the new product and treatments were mentioned, the American scientists and engineers who had developed the product swelled with pride. They called their campaign the "passionate plea."

When the "passionate plea" campaign hit the shop floor in Mexico, it didn't make much of a splash. Not because the people making the products didn't care about those they could help by working on the new production lines. They cared a lot about them. However, they cared even more about their own families back home who could not afford food let alone the most basic of health-care services.

As they watched the "passionate plea" campaign, they knew that their families and friends would never see the benefit of these great medical advances, so the campaign didn't move them to change their behavior.

The shop-floor workers were not chomping at the bit to learn the new equipment and processes simply because the campaign had been rolled out. What they cared about was more basic:

+ Was the new machinery more difficult to use?

+ Would it be more physically demanding to work on than their current machines?

+ Would the company still need the same number of shop-floor workers?

While the "passionate plea" had a place, it clearly didn't answer "What's in it for me?" for the production workers.

To truly connect with a change, it is important to appeal to both the head and the heart when helping make someone ready, willing and able to work on new products and in new ways. Just remember, the most important issue for people everywhere is, first and foremost, "What's in it for me?"

LOSING JOBS – WHEN IT GETS *REALLY* PERSONAL

It is always important to engage people's hearts when making change happen. However, when an organization is going to eliminate jobs, the nature of the connection changes.

When organizations go about changing, the impact on people is often an afterthought. Some leaders are so focused on achieving the change, they lose focus on how people are treated. The impact is on how smooth the transition is or how productive the organization will be.

There are two primary groups within your organization to consider when you are eliminating jobs: the people who will lose their jobs and the people who will be left behind.

If eliminating jobs does not take into account the needs of the people who are impacted, the gains you hope to make may be offset by large-scale disengagement, decreased productivity and massive turnover.

To say anyone is a "non-affected employee" during any downsizing or reduction in force is not accurate. During organizational transition, everyone is affected (even the leadership team). People who will lose their jobs are obviously impacted. What about the employees who don't lose jobs, may experience guilt that they "survived" and fear that they may be next?

How we help both groups transition is completely inter-related. For the "survivors," the #1 factor contributing to their experience in the transition is their observation of how those who lose jobs are treated.

If you are thinking about or are currently taking jobs out of the organization, some basic approaches will help you manage the transition for those leaving and staying.

First and foremost, the organization needs to treat people with respect and dignity throughout the process. It sounds easy enough, but it can be difficult in situations like this. We don't intend to treat people poorly, but sometimes we just forget about what individuals need, or we get busy and we forget about those impacted.

Every day, you need to ask yourself, "Is everything being done that I would want done if I was losing my job?"

As you make every decision, keep the Golden Rule in mind. How would you want to find out your job was being eliminated? Most likely, you'd like to hear it directly from your manager in a one-on-one conversation rather than in a meeting of 50 people. And you probably would want to hear it before anyone else in your group. While it is often logistically difficult, this effort will pay off.

Remember, the people who will lose jobs will likely remain friends with their former coworkers. If the people leaving the organization are treated poorly, you create ill will among ex-employees who bad-mouth your organization and also plant the seed with employees who stick around that they might not be treated so well, either.

Another key to success is sharing how difficult the situation is for all involved. Acknowledge it and don't be afraid to let others acknowledge it. **Communicate what you know, when you know it.**

Often, we are tempted to hold back information about job loss because we fear it will cause people to leave before we are ready to let them go. But, actually, if you give those who are about to lose their jobs more time to prepare, they will think they have been treated fairly. The people left behind will think their employer treats people with respect.

Sure, a few people may leave earlier than you'd like, but mostly you will end up with a team that knows leadership will treat them well.

The Golden Nuggets

✦ People make an emotional connection when they commit to new ways.

✦ Tacit communications and interactions can form the basis of what people truly believe and support.

✦ Connecting with people emotionally sometimes involves using influence and persuasion well.

✦ Appealing to the heart should take into consideration what it means for each individual.

GETTING TO THEIR HEARTS

Use this simplified stakeholder analysis to guide your thinking about stakeholders.

First, develop a comprehensive list of stakeholders and list them in the stakeholder analysis tool. To define stakeholders, answer the following questions:

✦ Who will be impacted by the change?

✦ Who will be the "customer" of the change?

✦ Who will be required to work differently?

✦ Who will provide inputs to the change?

✦ Who has influence over the change's success or failure?

✦ Who has formal authority over the groups impacted?

✦ Who has informal authority over the groups impacted?

Next, define what is important to the stakeholders and what or who the potential influencers are for each stakeholder.

Name	Role / Responsibility	What is important to them?	Influencers (what or who can connect with them?)

Adapted from *The Change Management Pocket Guide: Tools for Managing Change* © Change Guides LLC

CHAPTER 5

BEWARE THE PAPARAZZI

A leader's actions speak louder than words

In any organization, the leaders are the celebrities and the employees are the paparazzi. People watch what leaders do and say and then filter that information to figure out if they should support a change or not. Talking the talk is useless if walking the walk doesn't follow.

During times of major change, leaders are watched with even more scrutiny than usual. Change is the true test of a good leader. You may not see the flashbulbs, but people are watching.

Without effective leadership, organizations will not be successful at implementing change. When leaders are aligned and supportive of a change, there is success. When leaders are not aligned and supportive, there is failure ("Best Practices in Change Management," Prosci 2002, 2005).

It's really that simple. Leaders need to be aligned with their peers and supportive of change, and they need to understand how to show that support through their everyday actions.

LEADERS ARE THE CORE OF CHANGE

Leaders have a huge impact on change because people support what they *think* their leaders support. Here's the converse of this theory: If they don't think leaders are really going to make a change happen, they figure they shouldn't waste too much time or effort thinking about it. They think they have an "out" to just ignore it. If they duck down in their cube long enough, all of this change stuff will blow over.

For organizations that have tried to change and failed, people feel even more justified in believing they can wait it out and nothing will come of it or, if change does happen, it will probably be short-lived.

But how do people really know what a leader supports?

Certainly anyone in a leadership role is going to tell employees the big new thing is going to be great for the organization. But people develop their perceptions about what leaders support through the leaders' actions even more than their words. Doing what you say is the magic combination that moves people to act in new ways.

Leadership is certainly critical for organizations at any time, but leaders become even more vital during times of change.

When environments are changing around them, people work overtime to understand how things work and how they, the employees, fit in. During that time, people watch leaders more than they do at any other time ... and this scrutiny is intense.

If your organization is currently undergoing or contemplating a change, the focus should be on leadership. Specifically, there are two elements of leadership that are critical:

✦ **Alignment** – the extent to which leaders are on the same page about the change, why it's important, what it will mean to the organization.

✦ **Visible sponsorship** – what leaders are actually doing to demonstrate their support for the change, such as contributing resources, attending key meetings and encouraging others to work with the project team.

DEMONSTRATING VISIBLE SPONSORSHIP: PLAN THE WORK AND WORK THE PLAN

Leaders almost always are supportive of change, want to act as champions for change and guide people toward their vision. But many times these same leaders just don't have time or don't know how to do it.

A wise colleague once said, "It isn't real until it becomes a task in my Outlook calendar."

Demonstrating sponsorship is kind of like that. Once there is a task in someone's Outlook, the activity will likely happen and people will see support. Those tasks usually get done as long as they get scheduled into the very busy calendars of organizational leaders.

Small-yet-powerful activities can visibly show support of the change. But what are these small-yet-powerful activities?

Get involved in the change by attending project meetings, process reviews and workshops, hosting or kicking off a project event or making time to attend executive training. Making these change-related activities a priority on your calendar is a real signal that this is important.

Communicate about the change. Identify and tell people how the change strategy or vision guides their group's work. Follow up to ensure your communication is understood. Include change updates in regular staff meetings and hold "brown bag" lunches with your teams to identify and resolve concerns or issues.

Reward people for doing the right thing. Encourage people to get involved in project and initiative activities (process reviews, focus groups, etc.). Reward people's involvement in the change with public recognition or thank-you's. Maintain regular contact with full-time project team members who were part of their team, and develop a plan for them to re-enter your group when the project ends. Include project team members in regular staff meetings.

Walk the talk. When projects compete for time and resources, discuss them with your team and figure out how to effectively maintain support for the change's success. Include change-related objectives in your *personal* goals and objectives, as well as your team's personal goals and objectives. Offer up resources and support to the project team. Understand and expect resistance from people, and deal with it head on ... talk about it, raise issues, and try to resolve concerns. Don't pretend resistance or other issues don't exist.

Keep a positive attitude. Expect a learning curve and productivity dip while changes are put in place. Be patient. Maintain a positive outlook, even if the messages are negative.

Planning simple activities that demonstrate your support will be well worth the time and effort. Your organization will be on the right track when people impacted by the change consistently see their leaders visibly supporting the change.

DEMONSTRATING VISIBLE SPONSORSHIP: THE STUFF YOU JUST CAN'T SCHEDULE

The times when leaders are tested most is when they're not looking ... in a hallway conversation, a passing comment or even a facial expression during a team meeting.

If you are trying to effect change in your organization, watch what you do (or don't do), as well as what you say (or don't say). If an organization has some weaknesses within its leadership ranks, these need to be shored up quickly. And remember to smile for the paparazzi!

The following excerpt was adapted from the writings of Charles Galloway, an expert in non-verbal communication.

"The Man in the Mirror"

During many years of working with people in organizations at all levels, it is clear that leaders are capable observers of behavior. They are aware of behavioral meaning and its significance. At one time or another, leaders have remarked, "I notice how a person shakes hands, holds their posture, walks, listens, smiles, breaths, talks, and looks."

But herein lies a paradox. While leaders are busily looking and analyzing, they sometimes fail to comprehend what their own behaviors mean to others. Perhaps this is the occupational hazard of being the leader. Believing that they have the upper hand, they overestimate their power and authority, and underestimate the meaning of their expressions.

Leaders are instruments of change. In order to understand the meaning of their own behavior, they have to examine themselves. It is necessary to realize what they bring to any context may be more important than the so-called objective facts. When we read the behavior of others, we project our meanings and attitudes.

The greatest blocks and barriers to understanding may lie within us.

How does the leader initiate good communication and contacts with people? They must be willing to share their own perceptions and feelings with their staff based on what they see and understand. Their perceptions must not remain hidden. They have to trust the meaning of their own observations.

Likewise, they need to make it possible for others to talk to them about the meaning of the leader's actions. These exchanges must be viewed as worthwhile and necessary. Leaders must believe that living with the curtain open enhances the environment in which they work.

The "top executive's" sensitivity, willingness to communicate, and openness spread throughout an organization. If the leader doesn't share their perceptions and feelings, then it is hard for anyone else to find the courage to do it.

There is no such thing as non-behavior. There is no such thing as non-communication because the non-verbal is always there.

SLEEPING ON THE JOB ...
A Real Life Example

A president of a mid-size company began work 18 months ago to define how his new, more complex organization needed to operate. Month after month, he stood in staff meetings and pronounced emphatically that the new, more complex organization would mean that everyone would have to play at a higher level.

Leadership demanded excellence from every single employee. For the first few months, the monthly discussions got people excited about the future of their company and gave them pride in what they did and where they worked.

Then, this same company hired a young man as a manager in marketing. His task? To bring new ideas and energy to the group. Everyone liked him and he built strong relationships quickly. After a few months on the job, he started falling asleep at his desk on a regular basis ... literally asleep!

At first, people thought it was funny and they would put hats on him or move things around on his desk while he slept to surprise him when he woke up. But after a while, the situation became a pathetic joke.

Recently, a review of all of the functions across the company was done, and leaders were surprised to find that the productivity and creativity of the entire marketing department had dropped in the last six months.

Leaders realized that the message of "playing bigger" and "excellence" had been lost as people walked past their sleeping new hire. Clearly, the talk of excellence was just talk if the organization was going to let a sleeping dog lie. It was a hard lesson for leadership, but they finally got it. They fired the guy and owned up to the mistake. They also were honest about the fact that they should have acted sooner and that they, too, were learning how to take their company to the next level.

The organization recovered in time to make up for the temporary lag in productivity, and leaders built credibility and support from their staff in the process.

The Golden Nuggets

✦ Leading change requires the very best of every leader.

✦ Leaders must be aligned with what the change is and why it is important.

✦ Leaders must visibly support change.

✦ Leadership happens in small actions, not necessarily in large group meetings or major events.

WALKING THE TALK

Use this list with your leadership team to help them understand what they can do to demonstrate their support for the change:

UNDERSTAND AND TALK ABOUT THE VISION

+ Understand the business case and reasons "why" for the change.

+ Talk about the vision.

COMMUNICATE

+ Communicate "Why we are doing this?" to all employees.

+ Identify and communicate how the change affects your area's work.

+ Ensure cascade of strategy information to all employees in your group.

+ Use direct communication about the changes vs. delegating whenever possible .

+ Hold "brown bag" lunches to bring issues and concerns to the surface, then resolve them.

+ Follow up to ensure communication is understood.

+ Communicate a healthy mix of good news/bad news.

+ Include initiative updates in regular staff meetings.

+ Communicate the risk of not changing.

+ Discuss strategic scorecard progress against goals at checkpoint meetings.

SET AND MANAGE EXPECTATIONS

✦ Set realistic expectations.

✦ Allow employees adequate time for training and education.

✦ Expect a learning curve and productivity decreases during changes to new processes and technologies; be patient.

✦ Understand and expect resistance.

✦ Provide individual coaching as needed.

✦ Maintain a positive outlook, even if the message is negative.

PARTICIPATE

✦ Attend status meetings.

✦ Attend appropriate project meetings.

✦ Participate in project working sessions (i.e., process reviews, workshops).

✦ Host or kick off a project event (i.e., training).

✦ Attend executive training.

✦ Make activities related to the change a calendar priority.

✦ Get involved in the change project/initiative activities. such as kick offs and workshops.

✦ Encourage staff to get involved in project and initiative activities.

✦ Include project/initiative team members in your regular staff meetings.

✦ Be accessible to the project team.

DEMONSTRATE ACCOUNTABILITY

+ Include strategy-related objectives in personal development plans.

+ Hold the team accountable for results.

+ Be involved in critical decision-making.

+ Remove barriers or obstacles.

+ When issues or other changes compete for time and resources, work to effectively maintain support for the change's success.

TRACK AND REWARD RESULTS

+ Track progress of the team.

+ Reward team involvement and supportive behaviors with public and private recognition and "thanks".

YOU CAN SAY THAT AGAIN

Effective Communication Demands Quality and Quantity

Communicating during organizational change takes work, patience and courage.

Communicating during organizational change takes work, patience and courage.

Communicating during organizational change takes work, patience and courage.

Get the point?

Good communication takes strategy and planning. It includes determining what to communicate, how to communicate and who should communicate.

Managers and leaders need to be honest, take risks and engage their audience. They need to listen and respond. They need to do this over and over until the messages get through.

It takes organization, consistency and a continuous improvement mindset. Sound easy? Most organizations don't do it. They underestimate what it takes to communicate effectively. Although it takes effort, effective communication is worth it … and is a key element to successful organizational change.

BE HONEST

Managers don't have all the answers, but they get all the questions. In fact, many times employees think leaders have all the answers and just aren't sharing. The perception that leaders are withholding information must be broken if you are going to earn the audience's trust and get them to listen.

Being honest means telling them:

1) what you know,

2) what you don't know,

3) when you expect to have more information.

This is where leadership courage comes in.

Some people don't want to admit they don't have all the answers. If you are one of those people, get over it. Be a straight shooter and you will get their attention.

Even if you are honest, will they believe you? That hits on a bigger issue called *trust*. If you and your leadership have built trust by doing what you say and telling the truth, your employees − for the most part − will believe you.

If, on the other hand, you have a history of saying one thing and doing another, your communication may fall on deaf ears. Here's another twist: Maybe they trust you, but they know you're getting your information from leaders they don't trust. Bottom line, employees may not believe what you're saying in this case.

On the other hand, withholding information because you're concerned about the reaction is a bad strategy. Lack of information causes anxiety, especially if the upcoming change affects people's jobs. In these cases, it's even more important to communicate some of the downsides of the change.

For example, you may need to tell employees to expect a dip in productivity for a few months while everyone is getting used to the new process. By explaining the downside, it adds credibility to your communication. Even talking about a "worst-case scenario" helps people. Many times, the worse-case scenario is better than what fearful employees may be imagining.

Because we're human, sometimes when change is occurring, we make stuff up and rumors can go wild. You can't stop information from flowing, but you can influence what information your team or department is sharing.

BE ORGANIZED AND CONSISTENT

During times of change, a Communication Plan that is specific to the change is needed.

The Communication Plan for organizational change is a detailed listing of audiences, messages and communication vehicles necessary to build individual and organizational commitment. These approaches result in thoughtful, organized and audience-focused communication.

Working through a key message process assists in the communication strategy. This process helps you create consistent, relevant and motivating messages to communicate throughout the project.

During any change process, we encourage using the "message cascading" concept. Like a waterfall, communication needs to continually flow. The message cascading concept highlights the need for key messages that flow down to all affected levels of the organization. These messages answer questions like, "How does this project link to the department or organization goals and vision?" "Why should others care if this project succeeds?" and "What's the end result?"

It also may include asking, "What are the consequences if we fail?" These messages need to reach all stakeholders and should be reinforced at every opportunity and in every medium.

However, as the project progresses, other messages need to be added that are more stakeholder driven. Stakeholder groups usually have different issues and concerns, so they need targeted messages that address their specific needs. In addition, the level of detail in the messages will increase as more is known about the project. Messages about specific job changes, reporting relationships and job support will be added.

These stakeholder messages need to address "What's in it for me?" which may not be readily apparent. You will need to talk to stakeholders to understand their perspective, needs and what appeals to them about the change.

And, during the process of change, all messages need to be repeated ... again and again.

LISTEN AND RESPOND

All communication plans use a variety of methods to communicate – voicemails, newsletters, e-mails, meetings and one-on-one conversations. People within the organization need different types of communication at different points of time during their transition.

All these approaches are beneficial in times of change, but two-way communication **must** be part of the plan. Why? Because there are times that company-wide meetings and presentations are what people need. And then there are times when a one-on-one conversation with a boss or a roundtable conversation with peers works better.

In our consulting experience, we've seen too many organizations rely solely on large meetings and newsletters. Although these can be good for announcing a goal and reaching many people at the same time, they usually don't promote real understanding, nor are they conducive to two-way communication, which is most effective in times of change.

If done well, communicating about change begins an ongoing dialogue. Dialogue encourages questions and cultivates understanding. Dialogue also encourages trust and builds credibility.

When organizations change, gathering feedback may be the single most important communication element – and is usually the most ignored. Getting feedback from an audience is one way to see how effective (or ineffective) the communication strategy has been. It also focuses on what each audience believes to be most important in the change process.

Feedback can be gathered formally or informally and through verbal or written means. Once feedback has been collected, reviewed and analyzed, acting on the feedback gathered helps you improve your communication approach.

Here's the sticking point. Asking people for input takes courage. You may not like what people have to say. Even worse, you may not agree with what you're hearing or want to act on it. However, it is much better to know what people are thinking than to make assumptions. If you assume you know, you'll be wrong. No exceptions.

An effective communication plan includes written and face-to-face communication:

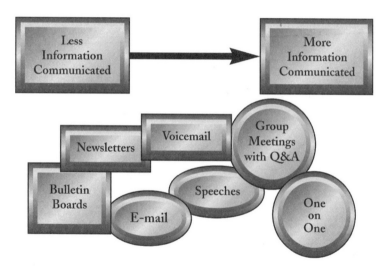

REMEMBER SYMBOLISM

Symbols convey meaning. They represent what is important, or in their absence, not important. Because people pay attention to symbols, they become one more tool of effective communication.

Sam Walton, founder of Wal-Mart, provides a great example of how symbolism works. Walton realized that he represented his company, so he did things to represent what he wanted his company to be. He wanted Wal-Mart to be seen as friendly, low cost and frugal with a focus on the customers.

Sam had his associates call him "Sam," not Mr. Walton. He usually wore a baseball cap and drove an old pickup truck. The furniture at the Wal-Mart headquarters was sparse and old. He did not believe money should be spent on things the customers wouldn't see.

Each of these symbols sent a powerful message to associates about what was and wasn't important in their culture.

In another example, one of our clients was trying to energize the work force that dressed unprofessionally and worked in an old, rundown building. He wanted to impress upon the staff that everything would be held to a higher standard.

How did he accomplish this? First, he moved them into a new, updated building and developed a dress code. These were symbols that the company was no longer conducting "business as usual." Things were changing.

Think about what symbols can be used within your organization when it comes time for change. They may not be as dramatic as Sam Walton's or those of our client, but your symbols can make an impact, just the same.

MAKE IT A GROUP ACTIVITY

Leaders who are aligned in support of a project and communicate that support are critical to an effective organization-wide strategy. A very effective strategy in this process is having stakeholder leaders who communicate updates and gather feedback.

We recommend creating a communication network – a group of stakeholders assigned communication responsibilities for the change in several organizations. This network serves to funnel accurate and timely information to employees and provides a way to send feedback and questions up through the communication chain.

Remember, communication isn't just about what is said but who says it.

SAY IT AGAIN AND AGAIN

If you've ever gone through the change process, chances are good you've heard frustrated leaders say, "We've told people again and again about why we are doing this, yet they don't seem to have a clue."

Why does this failure to understand occur? There are many reasons why it's hard to break through and get someone to listen and understand. One of the main reasons could be information overload, a problem caused by the barrage of voicemails and e-mails. Information overload is one of the biggest challenges organizations face when trying to communicate a message. Employees are bombarded daily.

To fix this problem, learn from what advertisers have known for years – an individual must be exposed to a message at least five times before they remember it.

You can also learn something from the fragrance industry – when sampling perfumes or colognes, most people get confused after trying three fragrances.

The lesson from both? There's a critical balance that must be achieved when communicating change. Avoid bombarding employees with too many messages because this only leads to confusion. However, provide the information through enough media so each employee will understand and remember the "why" of the change as well as what to expect in the way of results.

Communicating during organizational change takes work, patience and courage. With a coordinated, thoughtful communication strategy, people in the organization will start to understand why the change is needed, how they can play a role in that change and how they will be affected.

USING THE GRAPEVINE TO YOUR ADVANTAGE ...
A Real Life Example

One of our clients held a three-day retreat. It was the first such retreat in the history of the company and included 25 percent of the work force.

Near the end of the retreat, we spent time focusing on the communication strategy for the next day. Thirty retreat participants would be returning to "business as usual" the next day. But really, it wasn't going to be usual. Because of the novelty of the retreat, surely, the first question on the non-attending employees' lips would be, "How did the retreat go?"

How the participants chose to answer that question would have a big impact on how the non-attending employees would perceive the retreat. Those who didn't attend would be wondering, "Was it a good experience? Did everyone participate? What was decided ... and what's in it for me?"

If left to chance, those participants who attended the retreat may have answered in a consistent way, but then again, maybe not.

This is a perfect example of why it is important to have a thoughtful, consistent approach to organizational messages. It's important to take time to anticipate questions and think about responses. So, as part of the retreat, we spent time having the participants craft, discuss and eventually vote on the messages they thought were most important for their colleagues to hear.

The CEO called the next-day communication approach "using the grapevine."

Let's face it: Most people trust what their peers or friends say over someone in a different part or different level of the organization. Information is truly shared in the hallway, over a cup of coffee and in the lunchroom. It's those informal, frequent exchanges that make an impression.

So, picture an employee. He bumps into about six retreat participants over the course of that first day back. Each participant, in his or her own way, communicates that the retreat was a good experience, diverse opinions were heard, that strategic goals were agreed on, but the plans to reach the goals still needed to be formed. Lastly, every employee would have an opportunity to join a team to create those plans and make them a reality.

That is what we call effective communication and making a good impression.

The Golden Nuggets

✦ Communicating during organizational change takes work, patience and courage.

✦ A communication plan is an integral part of any successful change process.

✦ It's not just about WHAT is said, but WHO says it.

✦ Repeat, repeat, repeat.

Communication Audit

This exercise is an "as is" assessment of current organization communication strategies. Once the current approach is known, you can determine what can be leveraged and what needs to be added for your change communication plan to be effective.

1. Decide the method for data gathering (survey, focus groups, individual interviews or a combination) and the audience (entire organization or a representative sample).

2. Review the questions used to see if any should be deleted or if others should be added.

   a. How do you get information about your job and the organization (check all that apply): e-mail, voicemail, newsletter, department meetings, other (please specify)?

   b. How often do you get these communications?

c. Do you find this information useful? Why or why not?

d. Is information accurate?

e. How does information usually flow (top down, bottom up, by function, by levels)?

f. Is information about the state of the business and competition shared regularly? If so, how?

g. Is information shared freely between work groups? If so, how?

h. Are there formal feedback mechanisms such as discussion sessions, hotlines and comment cards? Please explain your answer.

i. Is the grapevine a good source of information? Please explain your answer.

3. Once you've collected the answers to these questions, determine what strengths can be leveraged and what weaknesses need to be addressed.

CHAPTER 7

IF *THEY* BUILD IT, *THEY* WILL COME

People support what they help create

True learning, commitment and understanding come from involvement and hands-on participation. The more people are involved in change, the less negative their inevitable reaction will be. People naturally support what they help create.

When it comes to involving others, there is a right way and a wrong way. Having someone sit quietly at a monthly meeting or worse yet – just having their name on a roster with no clear responsibilities – is not involvement. This may seem obvious, but we've seen it happen.

Truly involving others takes time, the ability to select the right people and the ability to delegate and manage diverse groups. Identifying various audiences and involving others the right way takes prioritization, inclusiveness and empowerment. The payoff for this approach is employee buy-in and commitment to the new strategy or goal. Remember, if they build it, they will come.

PAY ME NOW OR PAY ME LATER

People support what they help create. Here's a simple example to explain the concept:

A mom has a picky eater, so what should she do? The mom takes the toddler to the grocery store and lets the toddler pick out any food in the vegetable section. Once home, she asks her toddler to help make the green beans or mashed potatoes or salad. The assumption is that if the toddler picks out the food and helps make the food, he/she will be more likely to eat it. Many parenting magazines extol this approach.

At work, the same concept applies. If a process needs to be changed, ask the people currently doing the work to suggest changes. If a new strategy needs to be implemented, recruit those who will be impacted most to help plan.

This simple concept is used successfully in many environments. However, some companies use the "there's not enough time to involve people" excuse. The result is usually resistance and unmet timelines.

When it comes to investing time to build commitment, it's "pay me now or pay me later."

Let's see how this works. First, it is much better to have a proactive involvement strategy, slowing down at first (pay me now) to meet goals in the end. Compare this "pay-me-now" scenario to employees resisting an initiative because they don't understand it and aren't committed to it. This situation almost always builds ill will and usually requires going back to the drawing board or giving up ("pay me later").

PRIORITIZE GROUPS

Before deciding how to involve people, you need to decide who to involve. List the groups that will be impacted in some way by the change by asking these questions:

+ Who will be impacted by the change?

+ Who will be the "customer" of the change?

+ Who will be required to work differently?

+ Who will provide inputs to the change?

+ Who has influence over the change's success or failure?

+ Who has formal authority over the groups impacted?

+ Who has informal authority over the groups impacted?

Once these questions have been answered, start showing the list to others: leaders, colleagues, HR and internal experts. They will add to your list, and sometimes these lists grow to be several pages long!

Here's an example of how prioritizing works. Recently, we helped an organization with standardizing processes across seven independent-acting hospitals. They also were consolidating their operations into five buildings, closing two.

To begin making the list of who would be impacted by these changes, we thought about the people who work and visit those seven hospitals. Then, we added people who cared about the well being of these hospitals. The initial list quickly grew: patients, doctors, nurses, operations managers, the local government, the local media, board members and many departments, such as laboratory services and patient records, the university affiliated with the hospital and suppliers.

For this particular project, we eventually identified more than 20 groups. Notably, the list included both internal and external stakeholder groups. Not all of the groups required involvement, but they required some sort of communication.

The next step was to prioritize the groups. In this case, the employee groups, nurses and doctors were impacted the most and, therefore, needed to be involved. Targeted communication strategies were created for the rest.

Lastly, it is important to realize stakeholder lists tend to evolve during an initiative. The list needs to be reviewed and revised periodically, or as needed.

SLOW DOWN TO SPEED UP

Involving others slows down the process in the short term. It takes time to teach people about the project, its objectives and scope. Some refer to it as an "on boarding" process.

When people hear about the goals and rationale of change for the first time, they have questions. Some may be skeptical. However, taking the time to allow people to commit is critical to the success of the endeavor.

Bottom line, the change effort will not succeed if it is perceived to be a one-man show or an effort of a select few. It must be seen as a group process and, for this reason, any change process should be planned as an ever-growing effort that builds converts over time.

Once people are involved, they express their opinions and disagreements and raise new issues. This also slows things down.

However, all these activities are critical to building commitment and long-term project success.

In fact, the dialogue created by involving others promotes understanding, learning and commitment for everyone – even the leaders. It's also important to remember, not all decisions can be made by committee. However, decisions that affect the everyday work of an employee are usually better when they include input from those most affected.

LET GO TO GAIN GROUND

To build commitment, leaders and managers must delegate and empower stakeholders to make some of the decisions. Participating in decision-making builds commitment and ownership of the process and outcome.

Once you've decided what groups to involve, identify people capable of leading a team of stakeholders, someone who can influence and involve others. If you don't know who this could be, ask around for recommendations.

Also, ask stakeholder group leaders to choose other stakeholders to participate. Then, use these teams to tackle specific tasks.

Creating a new process? With the help of a trained facilitator, have the workers explain the current process and provide suggestions about how to improve it.

Using new technology? Have workers describe what the ideal computer screens and data access would be.

The workers involved in these activities will gain an understanding of what needs to change and why. Their commitment will increase as they participate and think that they are part of the solution. In turn, they will share their understanding with others. As the process moves forward, not only do the workers build their own commitment, but they start to help build understanding and commitment in others.

MANAGE THE GROWING FORCE

While it's relatively easy to manage our individual work or the work of a few people, involving others requires better project management skills. Involving others requires communicating timelines and updates, motivating the troops and rewarding their accomplishments.

Project milestones help those involved understand the deadlines and goals they are working toward. Using the milestones, it's important to take time to recognize hard work, team accomplishments and small wins. Recognition and reward always goes a long way in keeping people energized and motivated.

A good starting point is to develop a calendar, identifying dates when stakeholder leaders report progress to project management. This is one way the different groups can be up-to-date on each other's progress, issues and the need for collaboration across groups.

The people involved in change become ambassadors for the change. By effectively managing the project, you can make sure the rest of the staff or the team maintains confidence in the change. Why is this important? Because the confidence of your change ambassadors will seep down into the rest of the organization.

ONE DOWN, 724 TO GO ...
A Real Life Example

One of our clients was eliminating all of their separate computer programs and systems and replacing them with one system to serve the entire company. They needed to convert 725 geographically dispersed offices to this new, comprehensive system.

Once implemented, the workers could access more data. Their computer screens and how they input and used the data would be different.

The project would take several years, and leadership was concerned that the individual offices would perceive the project as another edict coming from headquarters. They also realized that a big key to success was to involve some of the office personnel from the beginning.

An office that was about an hour away from headquarters was chosen as the first to "go live." The office manager played a key role advising the project managers and communicating to her staff. Her staff shared the likes and dislikes of the current system and was instrumental in designing the training for all employees.

It took months of planning and incredible attention to detail to ensure the first "go live" office was committed and ready to go. However, it all paid off. That first "go live" went extremely well and was celebrated as an important milestone and win for both the project and the office.

As the change continued, the model used with that first office was slightly modified, then replicated with the other offices. The implementation continued to go well as all 700-plus offices adopted the change.

The Golden Nuggets

✦ A proactive involvement strategy slows things down but helps build the commitment necessary for success.

✦ Not everyone needs to be involved, but don't ignore any of the key players.

✦ Letting stakeholders make some of the decisions helps transfer ownership from the project.

STAKEHOLDER STRATEGIES LIST

Stakeholders can be involved in a change in many ways. In order to build commitment, consider asking them to do one of the following activities:

1. Lead a process-improvement team.

2. Participate in a process-improvement team.

3. Visit other facilities to gather benchmarking data.

4. Interview customers.

5. Help develop technology solutions.

6. Gather "as is" data.

7. Analyze data and make recommendations for improvement.

8. Present project information to peer stakeholders.

9. Gather feedback from peer stakeholders.

10. Write a guest column in the company newsletter.

11. Train people.

12. Work at a help desk or information line.

13. For communication purposes, offer their picture and testimonial in support of the change.

14. Attend outside training to increase expertise, then report back.

CHAPTER 8

YOU'RE NOT IN KANSAS ANYMORE

*Sustaining Change Takes
Support and Reinforcement*

"Toto, I've got a feeling we're not in Kansas anymore," Dorothy said in the *Wizard of Oz* (1939). Oz was clearly a different place. Not only did the green and glowing Oz look different from Kansas, but lions and scarecrows talked and munchkins, flying monkeys and witches roamed the world.

If an organization is striving to create its own new world, the individual transitions everyone has traveled need to be sustained.

Sustaining change takes a lot of work. You may already know this from past change experiences.

Let's say an organization does a big-bang implementation of a new way of working and training takes weeks of time away from the day-to-day business. The "go-live" is trumpeted with a big celebration and pats on the back abound. Then a few months later, the organization is right back where it started, except, of course, for the bucket of money that was spent implementing the change.

Support and reinforcement are critical for making changes stick. Without reinforcing new behaviors, people naturally revert back to old ways of working.

Want to avoid this ping-pong effect? By aligning systems and structures to reinforce new behaviors, you can help sustain gains made through change. To sustain change, the organization needs to have the right infrastructure in place to reinforce the change. In the end, the most successful organizations build a change competency so that they succeed in change over and over and over again.

PUTTING THE RIGHT INFRASTRUCTURE IN PLACE

In order to ensure that your desired changes yield sustainable and optimal results, new productive behaviors must be integrated into the way employees work.

In an ideal world, thinking about the way to support the new behaviors is part of the strategic change plan. It's not an after-thought that comes up after the project is over. But, problems seem to crop up after the project team is hard at work on their day-to-day jobs.

If not before, then, at the very least, after a change is put in place. An organization needs to look at how they are going to support and reinforce the new behaviors. Some of the questions include:

+ Who do we hire?

+ How do we train people?

✦ How are we organized?

✦ How do we evaluate and compensate people?

✦ How do we recognize people?

✦ How do we use information?

Sometimes, some of the old ways of hiring, developing and compensating people will work just fine in the new world. But often, the reinforcing systems in the organization are misaligned with the new behaviors.

People pay attention to what is evaluated and rewarded. If we ask people to do new work, but then we measure and reward them with the old metrics, don't be surprised if they revert back to doing what they were doing before. If, for example, you are measuring and rewarding people for speed, don't be surprised if you get a lot of stuff done fast.

A classic case of measurements and driving behaviors is sometimes seen in sales force compensation. If salespeople get a commission on gross sales, organizations get a lot of sales dollars. Not necessarily profit, but sales. In this environment, a committed salesperson is encouraged to get lots of sales, even if that means discounting more than the company would like.

The same is true with recruiting and development. If we ask people to do new work but then hire people based on the old job description and train in the old way, then behavior will revert back to the old ways.

SUSTAINING CHANGE ...
THE SECOND TIME'S THE CHARM ...
A Real Life Story

A small manufacturer was working to implement self-managed teams in its back office. The new way of working would require a much higher level of accountability from the staff ... a true stretch of their skills.

Their first try at implementing the changes went a little like this. The organization had a big kick-off meeting. During that meeting, the president announced plans for a new, exciting move to self-managed teams. The leaders divided all the workers into groups and told the managers to serve as problem-solvers and facilitators. The CEO also told the workers they now had more authority and they should take charge.

As a result, the managers ended up feeling threatened and the employees were bewildered. After a few months of everyone struggling to figure out what should be different, they gave up in frustration and went back to the old way of doing things.

Later, the president finally announced with defeat, "Self-managed teams just don't work for us."

A few months later, however, the president began thinking the process through again. Maybe it could work.

During a meeting with leaders from other companies, he was surprised to hear that others were having success with the concept. "We can't be that different," he thought.

Eventually, he decided to reach out to his colleagues at other companies to get some additional input and support. After talking it through with others, he realized the problem wasn't with the concept but, instead, with the lack of planning to support and sustain the change.

Announcing how things should be different wouldn't make it so, the CEO realized.

So, he went back to the drawing board. He analyzed the group's current systems and structures and asked himself:

+ Who do we hire?

+ What training and development do we provide for our people?

+ How are we organized?

+ How do we compensate people?

+ How do we evaluate performance?

+ What do we recognize and reward people for their work?

+ How do we use and share information?

Once he answered these and other questions, he asked himself, "What needs to change in order to support the self-managed team concept?" He recognized most of the things the organization was doing were counter to what was needed to reinforce a self-managed team environment. Almost every element of these systems and structures would need to change, including:

+ Creating training to build new skills in the current employees. Some of the new skills the workers needed to learn include working as a team, decision-making, scheduling, budgeting, communicating, hiring and evaluating. Managers need new skills, too, as they transition from a directive style to a supportive style.

+ Hiring employees with experience working in teams and with additional skills listed above in training.

+ Sharing more performance information with the teams.

+ Having teams use scheduling and budgeting software.

+ Eliminating a layer of management, thus creating a flatter organization. Managers who stay will have three teams to support instead of one. A workforce transition plan will be needed for managers whose positions are eliminated.

+ Including team achievement as part of evaluation, recognition and rewards

Creating the plans to support these changes took months. However, those months provided time for the CEO to communicate the benefits of the changes. There also was time to prepare and involve employees.

On the second go-around, the self-managed team initiative was successful. As expected, the transition took time, and some additional adjustments were made after implementation. But once they were made, the changes stuck. Each step of the change process had been structured, reinforced and supported so differently that doing it the old way was no longer an option.

GETTING GOOD AT CHANGE – AGAIN AND AGAIN...
If you can make change stick once, you've made a great start. But, given the pace of business change today and in the future, building a change management competency is going to be a clear competitive advantage for organizations.

Organizations that help their people move from thinking and acting in existing ways to thinking and acting in new ways are the organizations that are going to beat their competition every time.

In 2004, the research group Prosci developed and studied a "Change Management Maturity Model" that described different levels of skill that organizations must have to manage change ("Change Management Maturity Model," Prosci, 2004).

The report included the results of a survey of 180 organizations, commenting on how good they were at managing the human elements of change and how good they'd like to become.

Eighty-four percent of the respondents reported they didn't have a common approach or standards for managing the people element of change, let alone any significant organizational capability to manage change. An overwhelming 80 percent indicated they would like to have at least a common approach or standards to manage the people side of change. Even better, they wanted to make change management as a core competency for the organization.

What does it take to build an internal change management competency?

Some organizations, like Motorola and others, are building change management functions or centers of expertise. A team focusing only on the human elements of change ensures that it is not forgotten.

Many other organizations are developing or adopting common tools and techniques that can be used across an organization to manage change. Johnson & Johnson, for example, has their "Change Integration Process" and General Electric has their "Change Acceleration Process."

These and other organizations have learned that a common language and approach in managing the people aspect speeds along changing people's behavior. They also know that having a common set of tools helps get teams focused.

While developing a proprietary methodology and tool kit might make sense for large organizations, there are many methodologies and tools out there that companies can adopt without re-inventing the wheel.

Large consulting firms often bring their own tool kits to assist large clients, but smaller organizations can use and adapt to their particular environment without the need for consultants.

If you don't want to create your own model and you don't have the budget for consultants, find a model that fits your organization's sophistication and experience. Once you have a model, let people in the organization know what it is, why it is important and how to use it.

Teaching staff about a change management process and the tools needed to achieve change sends a powerful signal to employees that the people part of change is important. Skills, tools and common language will help them start doing the work.

Change management is the next frontier of business improvement for organizations of all sizes. Just as Six Sigma and Lean started with big companies, "trickled down" to smaller organizations and became a real competitive advantage for some, effectively managing change is starting to trickle.

If you can be ahead of the next guy by building an organization that manages people during change, your organization will be at the leading edge of success.

The Golden Nuggets

✦ Support and reinforcement are needed to sustain change.

✦ People pay attention to what is evaluated and rewarded.

✦ The right infrastructure (how the organization staffs, develops, trains, leads, etc.) will reinforce the new behaviors.

✦ Organizations that build an ongoing change competency will have the most long-term success.

ALIGNING SYSTEMS AND STRUCTURES

This systems-and-structures alignment matrix can be used to evaluate and address adaptations to ensure the organization's infrastructure can sustain change. Remember, systems and structures are organizational features, such as compensation, rewards/recognition, training, recruiting/staffing, organization structure and performance objectives.

Assess existing systems and structures by asking, "What do we do now?" and "What needs to be changed or added to reinforce the new behaviors?"

System/Structure	What do we do now?	What should be modified or added?
Measurements: How do we track performance?		
Rewards: How do we recognize and reward desired behaviors?		
Staffing: How do we acquire and place talent?		
Development: How do we build competence and capability?		
Communication: How do we use information to build and sustain momentum?		
Organization Structure: How are we organized today and how should we be organized in the future?		

Adapted from *The Change Management Pocket Guide: Tools for Managing Change* (Change Guides LLC, 2005)

WHAT WOULD YOU DO?

Putting it All to Work

In this section, we have provided a series of scenarios, one for each of the preceding chapters. The tools you've gleaned from your reading can be put to work. We've provided answers to the questions at the end of each scenario – **Answers to the Tough Questions**.

You may want to use these scenarios with your team or colleagues as role-play exercises to help others learn to confront the constants of change in action.

Chapter 1 – The False Start

The Project Team presented their recommendations to senior leadership. Leaders thought it was a brilliant presentation. With some minor modifications, the team's recommendations were poised to enter the implementation phase.

The Project Team diligently created a plan that would smooth out the flow of products from the manufacturing floor to the customer. They also created detailed "as-is" and "to-be" process maps, analyzing the amount of time they could cut from each step in the process. Finally, the team even recommended which jobs should be changed or eliminated to achieve the highest cost savings.

Six months after the project started, timelines started to slip and the budget was already at risk. Steve, a director who had just been hired from a competitor, was asked to take a look at what was happening. The leadership team knew his previous organization had been successful at doing some similar projects and figured he would have a fresh perspective.

In his short hallway conversations with team members, Steve learned a few things:

+ The team had built and tracked a sophisticated project workplan and budget.

+ The team was not getting the information and cooperation needed from employees who really knew the work better than anyone else.

+ The team was fighting a rumor that everyone in manufacturing was going to lose their jobs.

1. What questions should Steve ask to understand why the project is falling short of expectations?

2. What would you guess were some of the things that might be missing?

Chapter 2 – The Proposal Flops

The management meeting wasn't going well. Bob, a new hot-shot VP, was laying out the plan for the new organization structure he has worked on with the CEO.

He was getting a cool reception. No one in the room seemed to like his ideas. Mary, the VP of sales, said it would outright "ruin" the company. She also forecast a decline in sales, morale and effort since sales would be totally restructured.

1. How can Bob defuse Mary's outright resistance to his ideas?

2. In hindsight, what could Bob have done before the meeting to ensure the meeting would have gone better?

Chapter 3 – Good Grief ... Not Again!

John, the CEO, left the company meeting perplexed. He had just announced his exciting plans about launching a new project.

After making his announcement, John expected a lot of questions and excitement. Instead, the employees and even the management seemed unfazed.

John believed the company had built great momentum over the past year with many new projects. As he entered his office, Sheri, his VP of HR, came in. He asked her about the tepid reaction from the audience.

Sheri hesitated, not wanting to be the bearer of bad news. After he pressed her, she said that she heard a lot of grumblings about "not another new thing." She said people were getting tired of one announcement after another when they didn't think that things really ever changed.

1. What should John say to Sheri?

2. What could John have done differently?

Chapter 4 – "Will I Have a Job?"

JJ Juice and SodaPop Pop, two divisions of the same beverage manufacturer, had been working for three years to implement a common system and process to take and track customers' orders.

The customers who were ordering juice products from one division were often the same customers ordering carbonated drinks from the other.

The customers knew that JJ Juice and SodaPop Pop were part of the same corporation but had been setting up purchase orders and paying invoices separately for the two divisions for years.

In regular status meetings, Liz – the project director – kept hearing the team was running into issues with the customer-service groups in both divisions that did all of the order taking, tracking and invoicing.

Those groups would be impacted the most … and they had more information about the customers and the order-taking processes than anyone at the company. Their participation was critical!

Liz really started to get concerned about the customer-service groups. She was asked about a rumor that the company might not need two customer-service groups in the future and that customers could get all of their questions answered by one group.

1. What could Liz do about the situation?

2. What could Liz tell her team to do?

Chapter 5 – Confronting the Uncomfortable

Jeff was walking into the breakroom and saw his leadership peer, Isabelle, chatting with a few members of her staff. They looked like they were having a great time, laughing and joking, so Jeff decided to join them.

One of the guys said, "We're cracking up about the new forms that were just rolled out along with that new reporting system. We knew they were never going to get that new report system done by the deadline. It was only a matter of time before they crashed and burned and came back to us with a bunch of forms we have to fill out since the system doesn't work.

"Too bad no one wanted to listen," he continued. "I told that consultant guy when he came and asked us what we thought. I guess we weren't important enough to listen to … but we sure were right, weren't we!"

Isabelle and the guys again broke out in laughter.

Jeff was a little uncomfortable, but he just left the conversation with a shy smile and a nod.

Later in the day, Jeff had a long-standing meeting scheduled with Isabelle. He decided to ask her about the breakroom conversation. Jeff wanted to know why Isabelle never raised concerns about the reporting system completion date during any of the many leadership team. Why did she join in on the company bashing?

"I'm tired of us beating our heads against the wall," Isabelle responded with a sigh. "It's about time corporate realizes that a bunch of consulting suits can't come figure out all of our issues. We might not have MBAs from Harvard, but we know what we can do with the people we have. If a stupid reporting system was really that easy to put in and was going to fix all of our issues, we would have done it ourselves a long time ago. We knew the data wasn't good enough, and we told them that."

1. If you were Jeff, how would you start a conversation with Isabelle about the breakroom exchange?

2. If you were Jeff, how would you help Isabelle understand that there are ways to share concerns and vent about what is happening at the leadership levels?

Chapter 6 – The Uninvited Guest

Betty manages a group of nurses on third shift. Even though there had been newsletter articles and she had brought it up in meetings, she knew the nurses were barely aware of the upcoming changes in some of their daily processes – like lab ordering and discharging patients.

These new changes would require the use of new technology, and she knew this would feel radically different for most. In addition, she was concerned because the nurses had recently confided in her about their skepticism in hospital leadership. They felt the "suits" didn't understand what it really took to serve patients.

Betty had heard that the vice presidents were making the rounds to various departments to champion the changes. She was concerned her nurses would again feel like the "suits" were messing with their work and didn't understand.

While Betty was deep in thought, Sue, the vice president of nursing, approached her. "Betty, I was thinking about attending your next department meeting to announce our new process-improvement initiative. What do you think?"

1. How should Betty react?

2. What other preparation should Betty do to help ensure the announcement is successful?

Chapter 7 – Between a Rock and a Hard Place

The COO has called a meeting with Terry, who is the project manager on a process-improvement implementation. "We need this new approach working next month," barked Eric, the COO. "We don't have time to fool around. Our quality numbers are crap," he continued.

Terry had just started putting his team together after returning from a two-week, process-improvement course. The course had included a full day on change management. The instructors had convinced him that using a tactical, tool-driven approach to change management would work well when implementing process improvements.

Terry understood that they could not ram new processes down the workers' throats in a month. It would surely fail. On the other hand, Terry could feel the pressure from Eric bearing down on him.

1. How should Terry respond?

2. What's Terry's next step?

Chapter 8 – The Loose Ends

Outsourcing some of the basic HR functions was a great plan. Freeing up HR staff to do more strategic work with the business was in line with where the company and the industry were going. The program was called the "HR Transformation."

A team of the best and brightest HR staff outlined what types of work were transactional vs. strategic. They agreed on what work should be outsourced. They went through a diligent process of choosing the right vendor to work with, one who understood their industry and their employees.

Once the vendor was selected for most of the transactional work, it was time to get them up to speed and start transitioning work. But weeks turned into months and the HR staff seemed to still be doing all of the same old stuff. The VP of HR asked one of his most trusted directors, Sarah, to figure out what had happened and how to fix it.

1. What things could Sarah look at to see why people are not doing the new work?

2. What could Sarah tell the VP that needs to happen?

Answers to the Tough Questions

Chapter 1 – The False Start

What questions could Steve ask to understand why the project is falling short of expectations?

Steve could ask what has been communicated about the change already and what people are saying. If people do not think the change is important or how it will make things different, Steve will know he can get the project back on track by dealing with people and resistance. Steve also needs to know if leaders are giving the team the resources they need. If not, maybe leadership is not fully aligned on the importance of the change or is not demonstrating the sponsorship needed.

What would you guess were some of the things that might be missing?

People may be resisting the change. The vision may be unclear and there might not be enough or the right kind of communication. People might not understand what the change means to them personally. The leaders also may be unclear about the vision and unsure if they agree with the change or even know how important the change is.

Chapter 2 – The Proposal Flops

How can Bob defuse Mary's outright resistance to his ideas?

Bob could engage Mary in the process by meeting with her afterward to listen to her concerns. He also could ask her to join his implementation team. If Mary still doesn't seem engaged after a few meetings, Bob could ask the CEO to personally request support of the effort.

Bob also could tell Mary that her input is important and that he may consider some of her ideas about the sales-force structure.

In hindsight, what could Bob have done before the meeting to ensure it was successful?

Managing people through change takes time and effort, and a proactive strategy is best. Bob could have asked each VP for suggestions before a draft chart was created. He also could have met with each VP, shown them a draft organization chart and then asked for their reaction and their input.

Bob then could have gone a step further and asked each VP to present his or her part of the proposed organization chart. Using this strategy, the meeting would have felt more like a team effort instead of Bob was just telling them what to do.

Chapter 3 – Good Grief ... Not Again!

What could John say to Sheri?

John could tell her he appreciated her honesty because that is the only way to make future initiatives better. He probably wouldn't want to get the next new initiative started until he understands what is going on with the others. To gather this information, he could ask Sheri to arrange the meeting with his leadership staff to discuss what has gone well and what has gone poorly so they can learn from their mistakes.

What could John have done differently?

Some leaders assume past initiatives are taken care of by operational staff. They don't want to bother with the details. It's great to build on past successes, but it's just as important to understand past failures.

John could have achieved a better understanding of the status of past initiatives, asked his operational staff to give updates to the whole company and positioned this initiative in context of the others.

Chapter 4 – "Will I Have a Job?"

What could Liz do about the situation?

Liz could talk openly about the change, encouraging questions and being honest about what is known and what is not known. She also should let people know they could come to her directly with concerns.

Liz could spend time with the customer-service groups in small groups or in casual, one-on-one settings like breakfast or lunch gatherings. The relationships she built could help people connect to the change at a deeper level.

What could Liz tell her team to do?

She could let her team know that the customer-service groups need to care about this change on a deeper level – not just because it is going to be easier for the customers to place orders. She could encourage them to tackle questions openly, even if the answers are not known. And she could suggest that people on the team get to know the customer-service representatives and their concerns.

Chapter 5 – Confronting the Uncomfortable

How could Jeff start a conversation with Isabelle about the breakroom exchange?

Jeff could ask about her concerns and help her articulate specific issues. He could offer to help her frame her concerns so she could resolve them with the leadership team. Jeff also could ask Isabelle to bring issues to the leadership team rather than the staff, offering his help to do so.

How could Jeff help Isabelle understand that there are better ways to share her concerns and vent at the leadership levels?
Jeff could tell Isabelle her joking may signal to her staff that she isn't onboard with the change. He could discuss how the joking does not inspire them to accept the change and rise to the challenge. Jeff could encourage her to raise her concerns with people who can help fix them, rather than with those who don't control them. He could talk about how leaders lead with both their words and their actions.

Chapter 6 – The Uninvited Guest

How could Betty react?
Betty could accept her offer but do a few things to improve the chances of success. She could tell Sue she plans to speak and will try to get a nurse to come out in support as well. Having three people visibly supporting the change is better than the vice president doing it alone.

What other preparation should Betty do to help ensure the announcement is successful?
Betty should choose a nurse to speak who is well-respected by his or her peers and is usually supportive of new initiatives. Betty could tell the nurses in advance that the vice president of nursing is coming.

Chapter 7 – Between a Rock and a Hard Place

How could Terry respond?

Terry could emphasize his commitment to making this a successful, sustainable change. He could tell the COO that it's not possible to do it well in such a small amount of time. Knowing the COO values hard facts, Terry could explain the high failure rate of these types of projects when done too quickly. He could share some key take-aways he received during his recent training.

Terry also could ask the COO to add more staff to this important project.

What's Terry's next step?

Once people are chosen, Terry could ask the COO to give him one week. Then he could come back with a project team, plan and timeline he thinks will lead to success.

Chapter 8 – The Loose Ends

What things could Sarah consider when evaluating why people are not doing the new work?

Sarah could look at job descriptions and whether they had changed. She also could look at rewards and measures and the development programs for the HR staff.

If those factors have not changed since the HR Transformation, it is likely people are doing the same work in the same way. Sarah also could consider looking at whether people were trained to be "strategic partners" vs. administrators, and whether the organization structure supported these new roles.

What could Sarah tell the VP that needs to happen?

Sarah could tell the VP the new roles are very different from the past and that people need to be trained and rewarded. A good starting point would be training everyone on what it means to be a strategic business partner. Then, a thorough review of job descriptions, performance evaluations, compensation, career path and organization structure could be helpful.

The Pot of Gold

Chapter 1: It Takes a Village

- ✦ People make change work (or not work).

- ✦ People strive to re-establish control, understanding, support, and purpose during times of change.

- ✦ People develop commitment by going through. predictable stages.

Chapter 2: An Object at Rest Tends to Stay at Rest

- ✦ There are personal, structural and physiological reasons to resist change.

- ✦ People adopt change at different rates.

- ✦ Resistance must be brought out in the open so everyone can better understand and address the change-related challenges.

Chapter 3: Old Trees Have Deep Roots

- ✦ If employees perceive that nothing is wrong, nothing will change.

- ✦ The success or failure of past initiatives impacts how people view future initiatives.

- ✦ Culture can hinder or support change.

Chapter 4: **Get to the Heart of It**

- ✦ People make an emotional connection when they commit to new ways.

- ✦ Tacit communications and interactions can form the basis of what people truly believe and support.

- ✦ Connecting with people emotionally sometimes involves using influence and persuasion well.

- ✦ Appealing to the heart should take into consideration what it means for each individual.

Chapter 5: **Beware the Paparazzi**

- ✦ Leading change requires the very best of every leader.

- ✦ Leaders must be aligned with what the change is and why it is important.

- ✦ Leaders must visibly support change.

- ✦ Leadership happens in small actions, not necessarily in large group meetings or major events.

Chapter 6: **You Can Say That Again**

- ✦ Communicating during organizational change takes work, patience and courage.

- ✦ A communication plan is an integral part of any successful change process.

- ✦ It's not just about WHAT is said, but WHO says it.

- ✦ Repeat, repeat, repeat.

Chapter 7: **If They Build It, They Will Come**

+ A proactive involvement strategy slows things down but helps build the commitment necessary for success.

+ Not everyone needs to be involved, but don't ignore any of the key players.

+ Letting stakeholders make some of the decisions helps transfer ownership from the project.

Chapter 8: **You're Not in Kansas Anymore**

+ Support and reinforcement are needed to sustain change.

+ People pay attention to what is evaluated and rewarded.

+ The right infrastructure (how the organization staffs, develops, trains, leads, etc.) will reinforce the new behaviors.

+ Organizations that build an ongoing change competency will have the most long-term success.

ACKNOWLEDGEMENTS

Many people have contributed to the creation of this book. We would like to thank the countless clients and students we have worked with during our combined 30+ years of experience. They have helped us refine our thinking about change management. This book is richer because of our interactions and collaborations with them.

We would also like to thank the family, friends and colleagues who have supported us throughout the years. They have made it possible for us to learn and teach others about organizational change, and ultimately help organizations triumph over change.

About the Authors

Kate Nelson is a partner with Change Guides, LLC and co-author of the *Change Management Pocket Guide: Tools for Managing Change.* Kate has more than 15 years of experience working with organizations worldwide to help them manage change. Her clients have ranged from very small, privately held organizations and nonprofits to some of the world's largest multi-nationals. They have spanned many industries such as manufacturing, consumer products, and life sciences. Kate earned a BS from The College of William and Mary, an MBA from the Fisher School of Business and an MS from the School of Natural Resources at Ohio State University. She lives in Cincinnati, Ohio.

Stacy Aaron is a partner with Change Guides, LLC and co-author of the *Change Management Pocket Guide: Tools for Managing Change.* Stacy has more than 17 years of business experience specializing in change management, marketing and organizational behavior. Stacy has provided change management consulting and training to many health-care, service and manufacturing organizations. She has taught marketing at Miami University of Ohio and management and organizational behavior at Wilmington College. Stacy earned her MBA from the Weatherhead School of Management at Case Western Reserve University and lives in Cincinnati, Ohio.

About Change Guides

Change Guides LLC provides products and services that guide organizations through change. Founded in 2005 by Stacy Aaron and Kate Nelson, Change Guides helps companies and other consultants manage change and deal with the countless issues that come with integrating change into a workplace.

Change Guides offers some of these tools to help organizations manage change, including:

+ *The Change Management Pocket Guide: Tools for Managing Change* – In this pocket guide, there are 27 valuable change-management tools that can easily be customized for organizations.

+ **Electronic Tool Templates** – Electronic versions of the tools presented in the *Change Management Pocket Guide* **are available for purchase.** These Word and Excel templates are great companions to the book.

+ **Training** – Half-day and full-day training programs are available to support the rollout of change management within organizations. Training includes case studies to demonstrate how Change Guides tools have been applied at other companies.

+ **Certification** – The Change Agent Certification Program gives participants the resources and knowledge to confidently apply change-management principles and tools in their own organizations.

+ **Consulting/Coaching** – Consulting and coaching help manage change and use the Change Guides tools to their greatest advantage.

+ **Customization** – Many of the Change Guides tools can be customized to fit an organization's specific needs. Change Guides will customize the tools to maximize effectiveness for unique situations. Full licensing of Change Guides tools is also available.

To learn more about Change Guides, visit us at:
www.changeguidesllc.com.

Accelerate Personal Growth Package
$139.95

YES! Please send me extra copies of *The Eight Constants of Change!*
1-30 copies $14.95   31-100 copies $13.95   101+ copies $12.95

The Eight Constants of Change	___ copies X ___	= $ ___

Additional Personal Growth Resources

Accelerate Personal Growth Package	___ pack(s) X $139.95	= $ ___

(Includes one each of all items pictured on page 118.)

Other Books

_____	___ copies X ___	= $ ___
_____	___ copies X ___	= $ ___
_____	___ copies X ___	= $ ___
_____	___ copies X ___	= $ ___
_____	___ copies X ___	= $ ___
	Shipping & Handling	$ ___
	Subtotal	$ ___
	Sales Tax (8.25%-TX Only)	$ ___
	Total (U.S. Dollars Only)	**$ ___**

Shipping and Handling Charges

Total $ Amount	Up to $49	$50-$99	$100-$249	$250-$1199	$1200-$2999	$3000+
Charge	$7	$9	$16	$30	$80	$125

Name _____ Job Title _____

Organization _____ Phone _____

Shipping Address _____ Fax _____

Billing Address _____ E-mail _____
(required when ordering PowerPoint® Presentation)

City _____ State _____ ZIP _____

❑ Please invoice (Orders over $200) Purchase Order Number (if applicable) _____

Charge Your Order: ❑ MasterCard   ❑ Visa   ❑ American Express

Credit Card Number _____ Exp. Date _____

Signature _____

❑ Check Enclosed (Payable to: CornerStone Leadership)

Fax	**Mail**	**Phone**
972.274.2884	**P.O. Box 764087**	**888.789.5323**
	Dallas, TX 75376	

www.**CornerStoneLeadership**.com

Thank you for reading *The Eight Constants of Change*.
We hope it has assisted you in your quest for
personal and professional growth.

CornerStone Leadership is committed to provide new
and enlightening products to organizations worldwide.
Our mission is to fuel knowledge with practical resources
that will accelerate your team's productivity,
success and job satisfaction!

Best wishes for your continued success.

CornerStone
Leadership Institute
www.CornerStoneLeadership.com

Start a crusade in your organization –
have the courage to learn, the vision to lead,
and the passion to share.